Decodable Books Kindergarten, First and Second Grade

Orton Gillingham Decodable Readers for Early and Struggling Readers, and Students with Dyslexia
(Volume 1)

By Kate Mendoza

Table of Content

SECTION 1:
DECODABLE ILLUSTRATED STORIES (CVC WORDS)

SECTION 1:
DECODABLE ILLUSTRATED STORIES (CVC WORDS)

SECTION 2 :
CVC WORDS PHONEMIC AWARENESS ACTIVITIES

SECTION 3 :
IMPROVING COMPREHENSION WITH DECODABLE STORIES

YOUR FREE GIFTS

As a way of saying thanks for your purchase, I would like to offer you

TWO FREE complimentary resources:

- **Decodable Poem Set**: a collection of **illustrated poems** designed to help **early readers** practice **phonics skills** and improve reading fluency. Using decodable poems in early reading instruction can make the learning process **more engaging and enjoyable** for young learners.

- **CVC Word List Families with Illustrations**: a valuable resource for teachers, tutors, and homeschooling parents.

To get instant access just go to:

ecomclasse.com/free-gift

SCAN ME

Introduction

This book is part of the **Decodable Readers** series and has been specifically designed to help **early and struggling readers**, as well as students with **dyslexia**, improve their reading skills and gain confidence. With its unique focus on the **Orton Gillingham approach**, Decodable Books Kindergarten, First and Second Grade offers a proven and effective method for teaching reading that has helped countless children achieve success.

The **Decodable Readers** series contains a range of books, each with a different target reading skill. **This book (volume 1) focuses on short vowel sounds and CVC words**, making it an excellent choice for children who are just starting to learn to read. Other books in the series target different reading skills, such as long vowel sounds, consonant blends, and digraphs.

The book is divided into **3 sections**, each offering a unique and valuable learning experience:

❖ **Section 1** contains a **series of 9 engaging Decodable stories**, each accompanied by **fun illustrations** that are sure to captivate your child's imagination. These **CVC stories** will help your child develop their **decoding skills** and practice using **high-frequency sight words**, which are an important part of learning to read.

The hen was red.

the bug play in e sun.

❖ **Section 2** includes a range of **CVC phonemic awareness activities and games** that are specifically designed to help children develop their knowledge of **CVC words**. These activities are **interactive** and **fun**, and they will help your child understand how sounds relate to words.

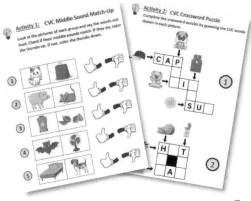

❖ Finally, in **<u>Section 3</u>**, you will find a range of **decodable stories** that have been specifically designed to **improve comprehension**. These stories will help your child develop their critical thinking skills and improve their overall reading comprehension.

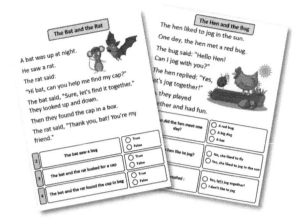

As a parent or tutor, you can use this book to help your child develop the necessary skills to become a proficient reader. You can use the book to create a structured and engaging reading program that focuses on phonics, phonemic awareness, and reading comprehension. The decodable stories and phonemic awareness activities in Section 1 and 2 can be used for individual or group instruction, allowing you to tailor the program to your child's specific needs. Section 3's decodable stories with comprehension questions can be used to assess your child's progress and provide opportunities for further discussion. By using the Orton Gillingham approach and the tools offered in **Decodable Books Kindergarten, First and Second Grade**, you will be providing your child with a solid foundation in reading, which will serve them well throughout their academic and professional lives.

Thank you for choosing **Decodable Books Kindergarten, First and Second Grade**, and we wish you and your child every success on this exciting learning adventure!

SECTION 1:
DECODABLE ILLUSTRATED STORIES (CVC WORDS)

Vowel Sound Targeted in Story 1: **Short a**

Featuring			
CVC Word list		**High-Frequency Sight Word List**	
Max	lap	and	the
cap	pat	a	on
fat	nap		
cat	has		
sat	had		
mat			

Max and the Cat

Max has a cap.

Max has a fat cat.

Max sat on a mat.

The cat sat on Max's lap.

Max pats the cat.

The cat had a nap.

Vowel Sound Targeted in Story 2: **Short a**

Featuring			
CVC Word list		**High-Frequency Sight Word List**	
rat	hat	a	the
had	jam	and	saw
ham	cat	said	
ran	bad		

The Cat and the Rat

A rat had a hat.

The rat had jam and ham.

The cat saw the rat.

The rat ran.

The cat said: bad rat!

Vowel Sound Targeted in Story 3: **Short e**

Featuring			
CVC Word list		**High-Frequency Sight Word List**	
Ken	met	and	the
hen	red	a	was
fed	pet	is	new
get	pen	in	its

Ken and the Hen

Ken met a hen.

The hen was red.

Ken fed the hen.

The hen is Ken's new pet.

Ken gets the hen in its pen.

Vowel Sound Targeted in Story 5: **Short i**

Featuring			
CVC Word list		**High-Frequency Sight Word List**	
Tim	pig	and	the
big	did	a	was
dig	six	gave	
fig	had		

Tim and the Pig

Tim had a pig.

The pig was big.

Tim did a dig.

Tim gave the pig six figs.

Vowel Sound Targeted in Story 6: **Short i**

Featuring			
CVC Word list		**High-Frequency Sight Word List**	
Vic	his	who	will
sis	Liz	and	with
hid	big	by	a
bin	him	not	see
did	win	said	

Who Will Win?

Vic played with his sis Liz.

Vic hid by a big bin.

Liz did not see him.

Vic said: Liz! I win!

Vowel Sound Targeted in Story 7: **Short o**

Featuring			
CVC Word list		**High-Frequency Sight Word List**	
Bob	dog	a	on
jog	lot	of	
hop	top		
log	has		

Bob's Dog

Bob has a dog.

Bob's dog jogs a lot.

Bob's dog hops on a top of a log.

Vowel Sound Targeted in Story 9: **Short u**

Featuring			
CVC Word list		**High-Frequency Sight Word List**	
Gus	pup	a	the
run	sun	in	play
mud	fun	and	
has	his		
had			

Fun in the Mud

Gus has a pup.

The pup runs in the sun.

Gus and the pup play in the mud.

Gus and his pup had fun.

Vowel Sound Targeted in Story 10: **Short u**

Featuring			
CVC Word list		**High-Frequency Sight Word List**	
pug	cup	a	the
rug	bug	on	is
hug	sun	and	play
has	sit	in	

The Pug and the Bug

A pug has a cup.

The pug sits on a rug.

A bug is on the rug

The pug hugs the bug.

The pug and the bug play in the sun.

Vowel Sound Targeted in Story 11: **All short vowels**

Featuring			
CVC Word list		**High-Frequency Sight Word List**	
Ben	has	a	of
lot	pet	and	is
cat	hen	the	in
pig	dog	its	to
fat	red	some	will
big	pug	well	
pen	run		
sun	can		
not	get		
vet	his		
dad	van		
med	pat		
nap	but		

Ben's Pets

Ben has a lot of pets.

Ben has a cat, a hen, a pig, and a dog.

The cat is fat, the hen is red.

The pig is big, the dog is a pug.

The hen is in its pen.

The cat and the dog run in the sun.

But the pig can not run.

Ben has to get the pig to the vet.

Ben and his dad get the pig
in the van.

The vet gets the pig some meds.

Ben pats the pig.

The pig has a nap.

The pig will get well.

SECTION 2 :
CVC WORDS PHONEMIC AWARENESS ACTIVITIES

 Activity 1   **CVC Middle Sound Match-Up**

 Activity 2   **CVC Crossword Puzzle**

Activity 1:   CVC Middle Sound Match-Up

Look at the pictures of each group and say the words out loud. Check if their middle sounds match. If they do, color the thumbs up. If not, color the thumbs down.

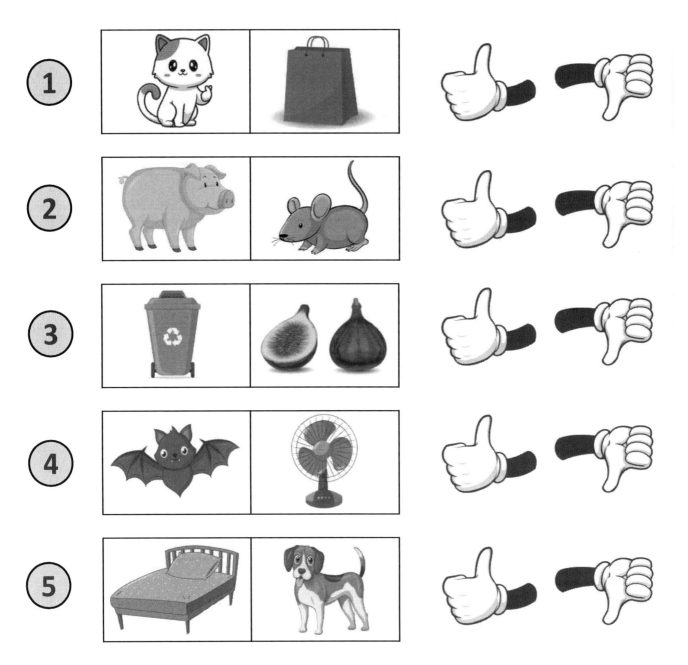

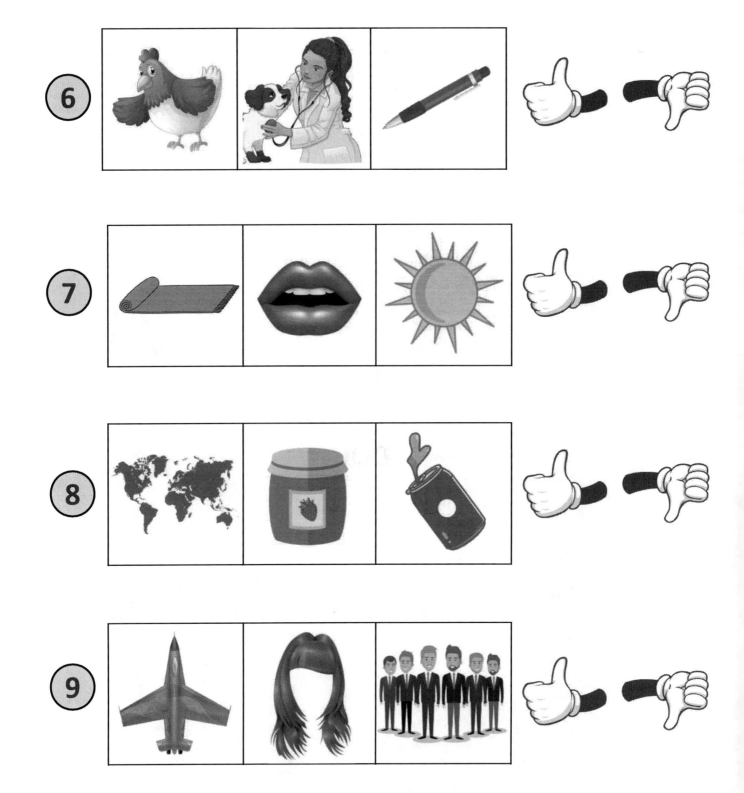

Activity 1: CVC Middle Sound Match-Up

Pictures key and solution

1	CAT	BAG	👍 👎
2	PIG	RAT	👍 👎
3	BIN	FIG	👍 👎
4	BAT	FAN	👍 👎
5	BED	DOG	👍 👎
6	HEN	VET	PEN	👍 👎
7	MAT	LIP	SUN	👍 👎
8	MAP	JAM	CAN	👍 👎
9	JET	WIG	MEN	👍 👎

Activity 2: CVC Crossword Puzzle

Complete the crossword puzzles by guessing the CVC words shown in each picture.

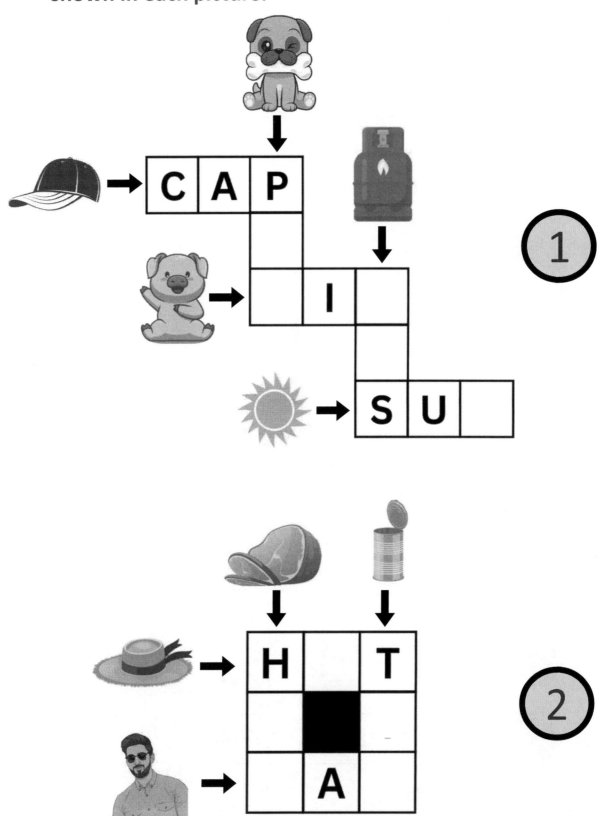

Crossword Puzzle Solutions

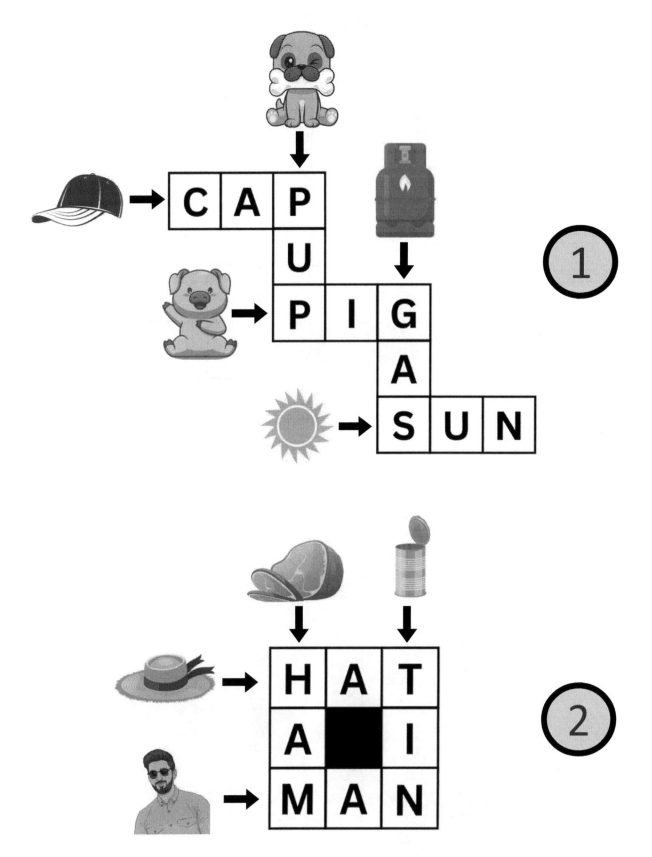

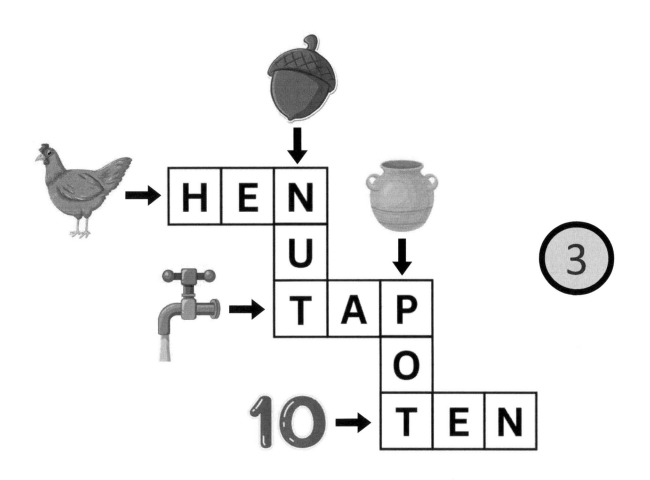

③

④

SECTION 3 :
IMPROVING COMPREHENSION WITH DECODABLE STORIES

Ben and Liz

Ben is six years old.

Liz is his sis.

She is ten years old.

Ben has a pet dog.

Liz has a fat cat.

The cat likes to nap all day.

The dog likes to run and play.

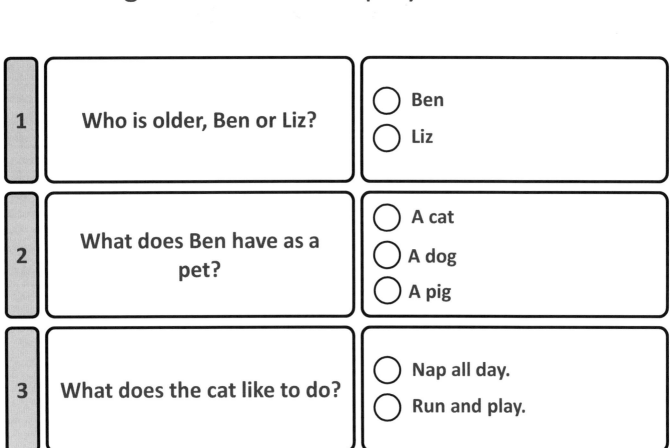

1	Who is older, Ben or Liz?	○ Ben ○ Liz
2	What does Ben have as a pet?	○ A cat ○ A dog ○ A pig
3	What does the cat like to do?	○ Nap all day. ○ Run and play.

The Hen and the Bug

The hen liked to jog in the sun.

One day, the hen met a red bug.

The bug said: "Hello Hen!
Can I jog with you?"

The hen replied: "Yes,
let's jog together!"

So, they played
together and had fun.

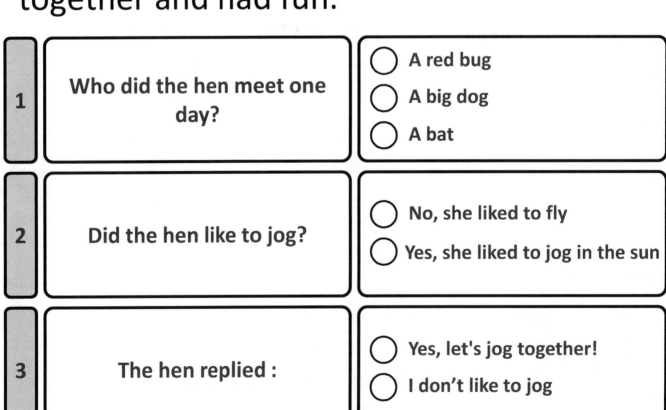

1	Who did the hen meet one day?	◯ A red bug ◯ A big dog ◯ A bat
2	Did the hen like to jog?	◯ No, she liked to fly ◯ Yes, she liked to jog in the sun
3	The hen replied :	◯ Yes, let's jog together! ◯ I don't like to jog

The Fox and the Pig

A fox sat on a log.

One day, he saw a pig.

The pig was fat.

The fox said:

Hi pig, run! a big hog is coming!

The pig hid in a keg.

The fox said: Pig! it was just a joke!

1	The fox sat on a log	○ True ○ False
2	The fox saw a hen	○ True ○ False
3	The pig was fat	○ True ○ False
4	The pig hid in a box	○ True ○ False

The Bat and the Rat

A bat was up at night.

He saw a rat.

The rat said:

Hi bat, can you help me find my cap?

The bat said, Sure, let's find it together. They looked up and down.

Then they found the cap in a box.

The rat said, Thank you, bat! You're my friend.

2	The bat saw a bug	○ True ○ False
3	The bat and the rat looked for a cap	○ True ○ False
4	The bat and the rat found the cap in bag	○ True ○ False

Answer Key for Comprehension Questions

Ben and Liz

1	Who is older, Ben or Liz?	( ) Ben (X) Liz
2	What does Ben have as a pet?	( ) A cat (X) A dog ( ) A pig
3	What does the cat like to do?	(X) Nap all day. ( ) Run and play.

The Hen and the Bug

1	Who did the hen meet one day?	(X) A red bug ( ) A big dog ( ) A bat
2	Did the hen like to jog?	( ) No, she liked to fly (X) Yes, she liked to jog in the sun
3	The hen replied :	(X) Yes, let's jog together! ( ) I don't like to jog

Answer Key for Comprehension Questions

The Fox and the Pig

1	The fox sat on a log	(X) True ( ) False
2	The fox saw a hen	( ) True (X) False
3	The pig was fat	(X) True ( ) False
4	The pig hid in a box	( ) True (X) False

The Bat and the Rat

1	The bat saw a bug	( ) True (X) False
2	The bat and the rat looked for a cap	(X) True ( ) False
3	The bat and the rat found the cap in bag	( ) True (X) False

Thank you very much for choosing my book.

You had many options, but you chose this one and I am truly grateful.

THANK YOU for taking the time to read it all the way through.

Before you go, I would like to kindly ask for a small favor. **Would you please consider leaving a review on Amazon? As an independent author, reviews are vital to help me continue creating the kind of books that make a difference for readers like you.**

Your feedback is valuable and means the world to me. Thank you again for your support, and I hope you enjoyed the book!

Leave a Review on Amazon US

Leave a Review on Amazon UK

If you are looking for more reading resources, I have a variety of decodable

Books available on my Amazon page:

Made in the USA
Middletown, DE
31 October 2023

41644050R00046